SHAKER FURNITURE:
A Craftsman's Journal

Timothy D. Rieman

SHAKER FURNITURE:
A Craftsman's Journal

Timothy D. Rieman

Library of Congress Cataloging-in-Publication Data:

Rieman, Timothy D.
   Shaker furniture : a craftsman's journal / Timothy D.
Rieman.
      p. cm.
   ISBN 0-7643-2445-4 (hardcover)
   1. Shaker furniture. 2. Furniture—United States—
History—19th century. I. Title.

NK2407.R544 2006
749.213088'288—dc22

2006001868

Type set in Americana XBd BT/Zurich BT

ISBN: 0-7643-2445-4
Printed in China

Back cover: tall clock courtesy of Suzanne Courcier and
Robert J. Wilkins

Published by Schiffer Publishing Ltd.
4880 Lower Valley Road
Atglen, PA 19310
Phone: (610) 593-1777;
Fax: (610) 593-2002
E-mail: Info@schifferbooks.com

For the largest selection of fine reference books
on this and related subjects, please visit our web
site at **www.schifferbooks.com**
We are always looking for people to write
books on new and related subjects. If you
have an idea for a book please contact us at
the above address.

This book may be purchased from the publisher.
Include $3.95 for shipping.
Please try your bookstore first.
You may write for a free catalog.

In Europe, Schiffer books are distributed by
Bushwood Books
6 Marksbury Ave.
Kew Gardens
Surrey TW9 4JF England
Phone: 44 (0) 20 8392-8585;
Fax: 44 (0) 20 8392-9876
E-mail: info@bushwoodbooks.co.uk
Free postage in the U.K., Europe; air mail at cost.

WALL CLOCK, MOUNT LEBANON, NEW YORK

Hancock Shaker Village

In his clock journal written in an idiosyncratic earthy narrative form, Brother Issac Newton Youngs tells of a series of time pieces he built in 1840 and the years that followed. Though his uncle Benjamin Youngs was a professionally trained clockmaker, Brother Isaac's clock movements were frankly quirky. He built clocks using the materials and the mechanical style of a tinkerer. Primarily self-taught, he was a man who worked on his own and in his own manner. His inimitable style is one of a uniquely reflective man who was known as a tailor, cabinetmaker, and most notably a scribe who did extensive writing about the Church family at Mount Lebanon. That Brother Issac was a clock maker may have been in itself a philosophical treatise on the meaning of time and timelessness of the human situation, for he, in his own way, spoke, or more specifically wrote, to issues wider than those of his own personal needs and yearnings.

Acknowledgments

I'd like to give a quick but sincere thank you to a few of those who have provided information, inspiration, and direction in my pursuit of life, meaning, and truth in the world of Shaker and the world at large. They are a disparate group. Some have provided guidance directly affecting this book, others in a much broader sphere of life. Again, thank you.

Ken Brown
Jerry Grant
Wallace Gustler
Barbara Kingsolver
Brother Arnold Hadd
T. Wayne Rieman
Paul Rochaleau
Stephen Stein
And others to be unnamed.

Contents

Preface

Shaker Furniture: A Craftsman's Journal is a visual tour of the master-pieces of Shaker furniture, with images for the eyes and for the mind. My personal journal, this text follows in concept the footsteps of Brother Freegift Wells from Watervliet, New York, a craftsman, mentor, and journalist who recorded thousands of daily entries, ranging from workshop activities and community events to the weather. *Shaker Furniture: A Craftsman's Journal* is not a technical treatise, but a personal narrative of the heart, intended to celebrate both the Shakers and the best of their plain and simple furniture.

I grew up a Hoosier, a flatlander of sorts, displaced by choice from my home in rural, Amish farmland in Indiana. Though I had been working in wood for years, I was new to the craft of the furniture maker. I was told by my parents that as a five-year-old kid I spent my allowance on nails, and Dad kept a supply of scrap wood from the lumberyard near the workbench in the basement for my twin brother and I to play with. By 1979, I was mostly a restoration carpenter and had rebuilt several houses, though my primary interest was the rural vernacular furniture found mostly at Amish farm auctions in the area. I knew of the Shakers through my search for alternative lifestyles and the book *Religion in Wood* by Faith and Edward Demming Andrews.

In addition, I was searching for a craftsman I could learn from, a modern apprentice-master craftsman relationship. When some friends dropped by my Airstream home in Indiana and suggested that I come with them to interview for an interpreter position at Hancock Shaker Village, I jumped at the opportunity. I got the job and worked in the wood working shop at Hancock interpreting, as best as a newcomer could, the furniture and crafts-manship of the Shakers. I was in a coveted position behind the barriers, with access to the furniture in room settings and in storage in the historic village. I was not aware of it to begin with, but I unwittingly developed a sort of apprenticeship with the Shaker craftsmen who had built their furniture a century ago, as I was immersed in the Shakers' furniture at Hancock and the Shaker Museum and Library nearby.

Most Shaker craftsmen, of course, had died well over a century ago. I'm not sure when I came to the realization of the relationship. It was not the kind of relationship that I had sought or envisioned, for I could not speak to my new teachers; their language was soft spoken, though eloquent, as they taught through the furniture they made and an occasional journal.

Few others took the time to seriously study the craftsman or their work. Few knew them by name. But I found that if I was willing to do serious examination and analysis, the Shaker craftsmen taught, in a concise though belated manner, through the furniture they had built. I needed to inspect, decipher, to unravel those mysteries that were overlooked with only cur-sory examination. I needed to question and to create hypotheses. I began to learn the trade, to differentiate and identify the furniture of some, and eventually, through their work, in a way I got to know many Shaker crafts-men – Amos Stewart, Grove Wright, Freegift Wells, Orren Haskins, Thomas

Damon, Henry Blinn, and others we will never be able to name. I was, I suppose, a begrudging learner at first, for it was something new for me, a new style of learning. But I became comfortable with it and, through hard work and requisite labor, I continued the ongoing search of the craft, the Shaker craftsman, and an understanding the fine furniture they built. In a few words, I would say, my life was changed.

Beyond my search of the craftsman's skills, I was drawn to the Shakers because of their communal lifestyle. As I explored their economic, community, and social structures, I tried to understand lives I had never lived. If any of us had been born in another era, in very different times, might we have found ourselves among the Believers? We never will know, but this does not prevent asking questions, and wanting to understand, and perhaps share the motivations, the dreams, and aspirations of those who lived, and continue to live, very different lives than we have lived.

This book was conceived in 1979 or '80 while I was at Hancock Shaker Village, though I was not cognizant of it at the time. Wanting to interpret well, I had so many questions about the Shaker craftsmen and their furniture. Few of my questions about Shaker furniture were answered by the books I read. I learned to respect the Shaker's furniture, inspected it carefully, crawled under and around hundreds of pieces, and built copies of pieces I loved but could never own. I compiled information, and began to take photographs. Chuck Muller and I coauthored *The Shaker Chair*, a book we intended to be a small seventy or eighty page book that grew into a much more serious and scholarly book as we found, compiled, and analyzed more and more information. Steve Metzger worked with us, contributing his fine line drawings and invaluable direction on book design and layout. Discussion, questions, and prodding by Jerry Grant continued to be influential in my work. *The Complete Book of Shaker Furniture* and its revision, *The Encyclopedia of Shaker Furniture*, with Jean Burks followed, based on my extensive analysis of the furniture, with craftsman and community attributions. Between these, I wrote *Shaker Furniture: Art of Craftsmanship* as The Mt. Lebanon Shaker Collection was studied and put on tour. Through all of this, my passion for book making was not fulfilled. As I appreciate the tools and the craft of my vocation – working in wood, I also enjoyed the tools and the craft of the bookmaker, and creating the images in the books I helped to write. A fabulous Linhof 4x5 camera, a Hasseblad, and a Contax 35 mm were my main tools, along with heavy bags of accessories, tripods, background paper, and old-fashioned tungsten lighting. Far from the snap shots of point and shoot cameras, many images took an hour, sometimes much more to compose, finding an image from the best perspective, relocating furniture, trying a different lens, or waiting for a cloud to pass. Many images required small apertures and exposures up to forty-five seconds in the low light in the Shaker buildings. Many photographs were taken, evaluated, and then retaken. Many were never used.

Over the past twenty-five years I accumulated a large file of Shaker furniture photographs – transparencies, snapshots, prints, and notes that admittedly have been much too haphazardly collected. An equally large mental file of images existed that begged to be more formally recorded and organized. This mental file changed over time, but a firm central core of the "best of" Shaker furniture always remained. This book is based on that small core of photographs and mental images, plus some images by several other fine contemporary photographers. Photographs of numerous known and unknown historic photographers were used to provide both visual and historical context. I chose to restrict the book to a group of about sixty pieces of furniture. Yes, others of equal quality could have been included but by whim, erroneous choice or necessity, were not.

The objects of this book are not fine oil paintings, classical sculptures, or Egyptian artifacts. These Shaker furniture masterpieces are instead basic objects, simple furniture created by and surrounded by an important religious sect still alive – the Shakers, who came to life in the latter part of the eighteenth century. Yes, the masterpieces are those basic objects that resided in the periphery of ordinary and extraordinary people's lives, and helped define the perimeter of their work and living spaces. They are those objects Shakers sat on, where they placed their eating utensils and ate their meals, and those objects that provided storage or the work surfaces to sit or stand at to accomplish daily tasks … plain and simple furniture.

Often the perspective of an observer determines the lasting image of an object. The photographs of William Winter used by Faith and Edward Demming Andrews in *Shaker Furniture* and *Religion in Wood* provided a distinctive style and perspective of seeing Shaker furniture. The Shaker Furniture, as described by Jerry Grant and Hugh Howard in *The Eastfield Record* was set in sparsely arranged rooms to provide an image the Andrews sought, at times denying the present reality. The images by the photographer Winter set a tone of how Shaker furniture and their living spaces were viewed until the 1980s. The book *Shaker Design,* by June Spriggs, with the fine photographs of Paul Rochaleau, emerged in 1986. In *Shaker Design,* the furniture was visually isolated on the white page, connected to the Shakers only by the text, providing a nearly sterile perspective to see an object nearly entirely from a design or artistic perspective. This ability to create an image is of course within the realm of the photographer, to stop time in the process of recording an image on film. It is in that moment that one image is recorded, only one of an infinitesimal number that could have been preserved, each providing a different visual and emotive perspective.

In *Shaker Furniture: A Craftsman's Journal*, I have chosen to visually connect a piece with its historic context, attempting to answer, or perhaps more often ask, philosophical questions – where was it created, who used it, in what setting? For example, the 1837 new attic at Canterbury is situated on a page spread with the building where this amazing complex of built-ins exists. In another I place a historic photographic of a Sister dressed in a Shaker handmade dress next to a work table or counter, of the type likely to have been used to layout, cut, and assemble it. Some pieces are isolated, as if on a pedestal to be viewed apart from everything around it. Other pieces are presented with detail photos to provide a specific focus.

Alas, all of these images are isolated from the living Shaker community, even though many were taken in Shaker buildings. I have tried to retain some fleeting connection with the Shakers through the use of captions and historic photographs. The reality exists though, that with the exception of furniture still in daily use at Sabbathday Lake community in Maine, these objects are removed from the everyday life of the Shakers, removed from their real life setting, and the reasons they were created, distancing the observer from understanding the object. Something is inevitably lost.

I want to acknowledge that these objects, Shaker furniture, part of the physical output of the Shakers, represent but one exceedingly small part of Shaker life. Far more important is the Shakers continued contribution to the strength and spirit of communal religious life, as these courageous people continue to live their lives.

Timothy D. Rieman

Introduction

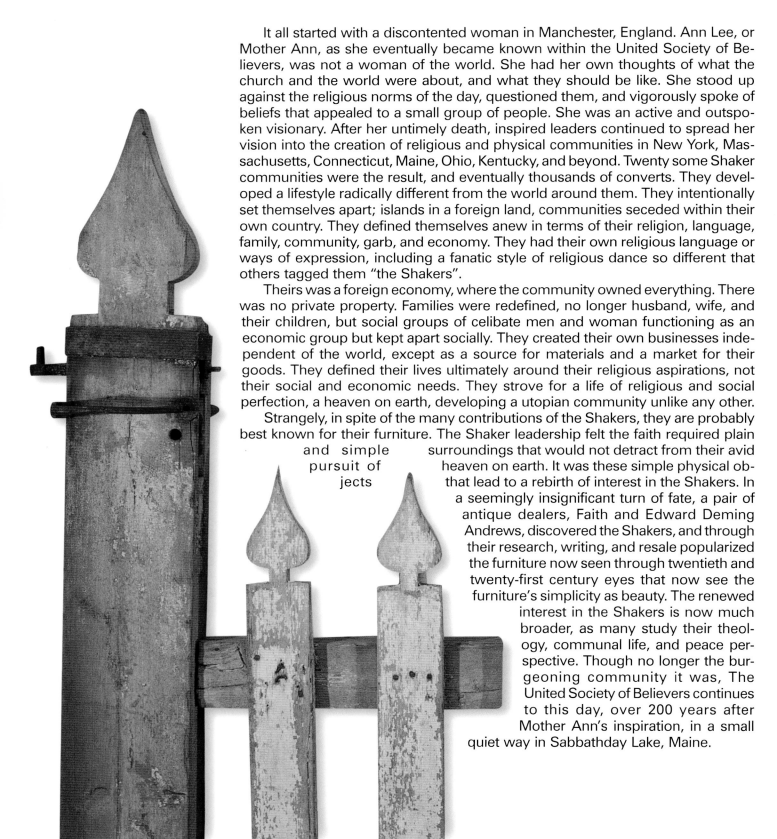

It all started with a discontented woman in Manchester, England. Ann Lee, or Mother Ann, as she eventually became known within the United Society of Believers, was not a woman of the world. She had her own thoughts of what the church and the world were about, and what they should be like. She stood up against the religious norms of the day, questioned them, and vigorously spoke of beliefs that appealed to a small group of people. She was an active and outspoken visionary. After her untimely death, inspired leaders continued to spread her vision into the creation of religious and physical communities in New York, Massachusetts, Connecticut, Maine, Ohio, Kentucky, and beyond. Twenty some Shaker communities were the result, and eventually thousands of converts. They developed a lifestyle radically different from the world around them. They intentionally set themselves apart; islands in a foreign land, communities seceded within their own country. They defined themselves anew in terms of their religion, language, family, community, garb, and economy. They had their own religious language or ways of expression, including a fanatic style of religious dance so different that others tagged them "the Shakers".

Theirs was a foreign economy, where the community owned everything. There was no private property. Families were redefined, no longer husband, wife, and their children, but social groups of celibate men and woman functioning as an economic group but kept apart socially. They created their own businesses independent of the world, except as a source for materials and a market for their goods. They defined their lives ultimately around their religious aspirations, not their social and economic needs. They strove for a life of religious and social perfection, a heaven on earth, developing a utopian community unlike any other.

Strangely, in spite of the many contributions of the Shakers, they are probably best known for their furniture. The Shaker leadership felt the faith required plain and simple surroundings that would not detract from their avid pursuit of heaven on earth. It was these simple physical objects that lead to a rebirth of interest in the Shakers. In a seemingly insignificant turn of fate, a pair of antique dealers, Faith and Edward Deming Andrews, discovered the Shakers, and through their research, writing, and resale popularized the furniture now seen through twentieth and twenty-first century eyes that now see the furniture's simplicity as beauty. The renewed interest in the Shakers is now much broader, as many study their theology, communal life, and peace perspective. Though no longer the burgeoning community it was, The United Society of Believers continues to this day, over 200 years after Mother Ann's inspiration, in a small quiet way in Sabbathday Lake, Maine.

13

15

The Craftsman's Journal

MOUNT LEBANON, NEW YORK, SHAKER SOCIETY'S SPIRITUAL HEADQUARTERS

Built into the western facing mountainside, Mount Lebanon was once a vibrant community of over 500 Believers. Housing the central ministry, it set the direction and standards of the United Society. About thirty buildings remain, reconstituted for a second life, and are now used by a Sufi community (an Eastern alternative culture), individual family residences, and a private high school with the academic culture of a school sharing its theater, rock music, and hillside sun tans. At the extreme northern end of the original Shaker village site, the immense stone walls of the North Family barn emerge from the hillside like Mayan ruins. They provide clear evidence of the continuum of cultures, one of the past rapidly declining, the other still growing and not yet knowing reasonable bounds. Both cultures inhabit the same space, though they are many decades and mind sets apart. Plans for the North Family site's renewal and reconstruction of the barn still (as of December 2005) lay rolled up in long white cylinders – blue prints for new exhibition space for the fine collection of the Shaker Museum and Library that is moving to the site. Within earshot just up hill, US 20, overloaded with cars and semis, leads traffic traversing new asphalt pavement laid on the side of the Taconic mountain range where early twentieth century photographic views portrayed a mountainside of pasture and open fields. Much of the site is now re-enveloped by forest lands, as it was before the Shakers inhabited the land, though the forests compete with many new homes and the real estate firms advertising mountainside views of the valley. In spite of the numerous changes, somehow the beauty and spirit of the site still exists, even though the Shakers left over half a century ago.

1. Church family meetinghouse
2. N. family barn
3. Canaan family
4. Mount Lebanon from the South
5. Church family
6. Center family
7. North family

BROTHERS – WORKERS IN WOOD

One can only imagine how the lives of so many men were changed and enriched as they chose to become Believers. There were many and varied reasons for joining, among them the strong Shaker religious tenants, the strength of community, extended family relationships, and economic security. Some left the Shakers after living there for only a few years, unable to adjust to the rigors of a life very different from the one they came from. Yet many became life-long Believers, perhaps hearing a different drummer, seeking a much different, smaller – or was it larger – world than the one they left behind. These are but some of the believers, brothers who worked in wood and who brushed the sawdust and shavings off their clothing at the end of their work day.

1. Henry Green
2. Delmar Wilson
3. Henry Blinn
4. Robert Wagan
5. Amos Stewart
6. Giles Avery
7. Orren Haskins
The brother just left of center in front row

Shaker Museum and Library

Richard Brooker

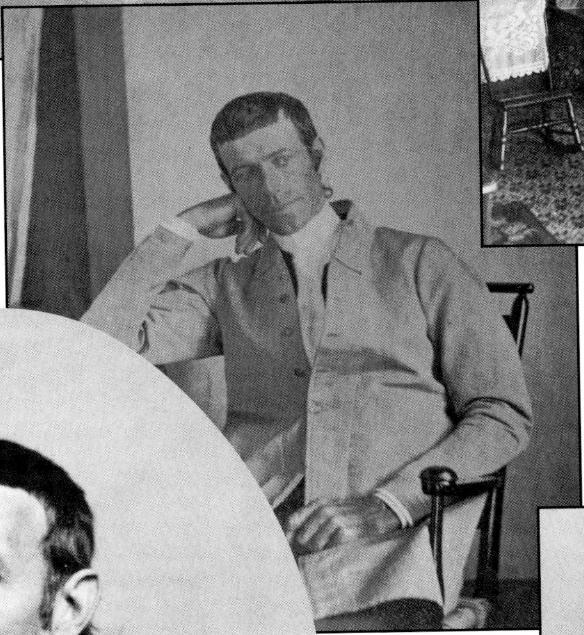

Shaker Museum and Library

Shaker Museum and Library

Shaker Museum and Library

COLOR

Resplendent in their use of color, the Shakers' living spaces were not what many today would have expected to see. Bold or subtle hues and shades in blue, yellow, red, and green, and the natural colors of varnished wood were highlighted by the expanses of white plaster walls framed by varnished or painted door and window trim and yards of horizontal peg rails. The depth and color of some capture the depth of the sunset hues, warm, rich, and vibrant. Basic pigments were used in their paint formulations like red ocher, chrome yellow, verdigris green, yellow ochre, and Prussian blue, along with red and white lead that altered these colors. These pigments varied considerably, depending on the source and where it was mined and processed. The nuances are infinite, with deep beautiful colors that haven't been named yet even by our twenty-first century paint companies with their imaginative but meaningless names like moon rise, wild porcini, evening symphony, and twilight dusk. The paint color was, of course, not static. The inescapable change echoes the northeastern fall foliage that moves inexorably from vibrant and variable reds and yellows to a more subdued or mellow color, becoming quieter and softer following their long seasonal pilgrimage of color. The visual change of the painted furniture is, of course, understood through vastly different scientific perspectives and takes place over decades or centuries rather than the few fleeting weeks of fall.

FUNCTION, FORM, FAÇADE

The primary architects of Shaker design were the furniture makers. Though both written and unwritten regulations or standards existed defining the concept of "plain and simple", somehow the delicate dynamic balance between rigid regulations and artistic license was found between the hierarchical central ministry and the individual craftsman. The craftsmen, the workers in wood, created and crafted the furniture designs transforming the concept of plain and simple into the reality of Shaker furniture, creating "Shaker design" as we know it today. The craftsmen eliminated extraneous detail, but retained a minimalist ornamentation, a small cornice, a curved line, a beaded edge. They developed a common sense that enabled them to draw the line between the purely functional and the excessively decorative. The dichotomy of community and regional differences existed counter-posed with the similarities that tied the common threads of a homogenous Shaker design. The Shakers, as they were developing as a sect in the 1780s to 1800 in the new United States, were in many ways foreigners in their own country. They posed a radically different lifestyle to those around them. They spoke a different religious language, held to opposing family structures of brother and sister rather than husband and wife, and withdrew from many of their connections with their local communities. It can therefore reasonably be expected that their physical surroundings, their buildings, and furniture would differ from their neighbors. Several basic furniture forms were used by Shaker craftsmen: cupboard, case of drawers, counter, sewing case, three- and four-leg tables, trestle tables, and chairs. These forms were refined by the variations in proportion, arrangement, symmetry, size, and decorative details which were most likely chosen by the builder. Each was designed to fill a specific need and fit a particular space.

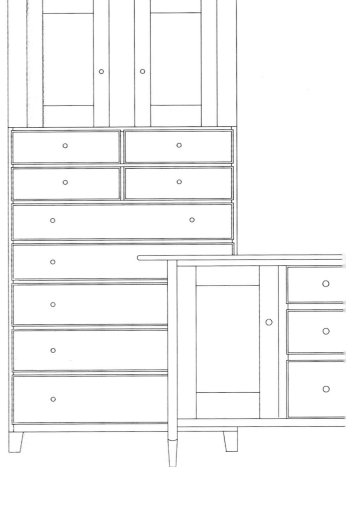

24

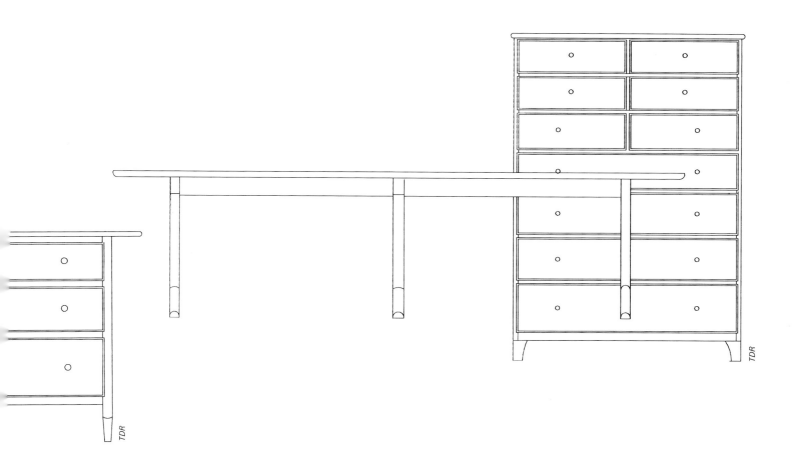

WORKBENCH, MOUNT LEBANON, NEW YORK

Hancock Shaker Village

The workbench is the most basic of the cabinetmaker's tools. More than a simple work surface for layout work and assembly, it has vices to secure stock for mortise and tenon work or dovetailing, and an end vice and dogs to hold planks that allow the cabinetmaker to plane the broad surfaces or planks for the Shakers' massive cabinetry. This bench is certainly among the most notable of the Shakers' workbenches. It is not the largest or the longest, nor does it have the most drawers or cupboards. It remains, however, one of the most aesthetically memorable benches as the base retains much of its now well-worn blue and black paint below the varnished top. Remarkably, quite a few of the Shakers workbenches exist, many in museums. Others, maybe because they are so incredibly heavy and difficult to move, reside dust covered and unused in poorly heated outbuildings. They are unused too because so few, even of the best of craftsmen today, know the use of a finely sharpened smoothing plane being pushed over a plank secured between a pair of bench dogs on a low, old fashioned workbench. Few know the feeling of a paper thin shaving streaming from the throat of a plane as a plank is fashioned into its destiny, a cupboard panel or the side of a case of drawers. Few know the need to push the ankle deep piles of curled shavings to the side of the workspace to allow for more work to be done. Brother Charles Greaves, pictured here, may have seen the workshops in his earlier years around the Shaker village. Though he was not known as a craftsman, he appears in this historic photograph with the tools of a woodworker.

Shaker Museum and Library

Hancock Shaker Village

Like guardians to a communal history unknown to most of us from the world, these built-ins stood witness to Shaker life for 130 years. Built into the 1830 Hancock Church Family Dwelling, butternut built-in storage units like these, with façades of various arrangements, were integrated into nearly every room. Most were located in retiring rooms for the storage of clothing and bedding. Others found in the meeting and dining rooms, hallways, and kitchen were built to serve specific storage requirements. Originally most were finished with contrasting red and yellow paint but now stand with an old, more subdued varnished finish. The Church Family Dwelling was designed to house 80 to 100 Believers. Elder Grove Wright was integrally involved in the construction of the casework in the communal building. Though his work there was not signed, other known furniture, handwriting style, and the construction details including the unique tapering of drawer sides, point to his fine workmanship throughout much of the brick structure. The historic photograph shows several believers posed on the steps of the dwelling facing the road leading into Pittsfield to the east or New Lebanon to the west across the Taconic Mountains.

A. J. Alden, Hancock Shaker Village

Church Family Album, Hancock Shaker Village

BUILT-IN CABINETRY, HARVARD, MASSACHUSETTS

Private Collection

Some seeking religious perfection in eastern Massachusetts found the town of Harvard a gathering point. There Mother Ann Lee and other Shaker missionaries visited on numerous itinerant evangelistic journeys. The Shakers found receptive and fertile minds, and eventually two Shaker communities were created, Harvard and nearby Shirley. The Shaker sisters portrayed here were, of course, not of that early group, but were, in a sense, pilgrims in the Shaker way decades later. Many buildings were built as the Harvard community developed. Within one in particular, expansive arrays of built-ins were created. Like a modern sculpture balanced in its own unique manner, this particular assemblage of cupboards and drawers has a logic that is unseen until one explores further beyond the façade. Between two walls, a stairway leading downward from left to right, created an unusual space that was well utilized by an efficient Harvard cabinetmaker in the Church Family Dwelling. There is another room beyond the stairway that contains an arrangement similar to this one. Was the craftsman cognizant of the intriguing asymmetry of his cabinetry or was it constructed totally from an efficient utilitarian perspective?

Private Collection

Hancock Shaker Village

BUILT-IN CABINTRY, PLEASANT HILL, KENTUCKY

Shaker Village at Pleasant Hill, Kentucky

Beautifully conceived in its construction, function, and visual presence, this storage space is located in the attic of the Centre family dwelling. Though unique in its U-shaped arrangement, this attic storage unit emerged from a regional and Shaker design tradition. Kentucky Shaker cabinetmakers routinely used cherry as a primary wood, and constructed pieces with substantial frame and panel casework. This example makes an obvious use of pattern in the replication of one similar five drawer case after another. In fact though, a much more basic pattern exists, quickly overlooked by our minds eye, as we move from one thing to another. More easily seen during the earlier stages of the construction process without the drawers in place, is the simple grid like structure of the case face, where the horizontal rails between drawers are secured incrementally by the vertical stiles that separate each bank of drawers. Balancing the rigid rectilinear shapes are paired knobs on each drawer face. Maybe a day or two of work for a skilled turner, the ninety knobs are as close to identical as the eye can see. Each evolved from the spinning stock with the manipulative touch of the turners steel gouge on the craftsman's lathe.

Shaker Museum and Library

Shaker Museum and Library

44

CUPBOARD OVER CASE OF DRAWERS, MOUNT LEBANON, NEW YORK

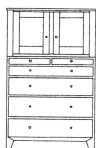
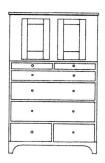

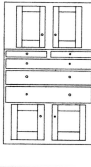
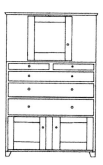

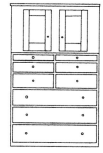

Shaker Museum and Library

Rarely do we know which Shaker Brother or Sister used a specific piece of furniture. This classic 1830 cupboard over drawers is one exception. Oral history tells us that this piece was used by Sister Emma Jane Neale, who is seated in the historic photograph with her natural sister Sadie. Born in 1847, Sister Emma was involved in teaching children in the Shaker school. She also served as Trustee at Mount Lebanon for more than fifty years. For three decades she provided leadership in the cloak industry, marketing their flowing garments under the "company" name of Emma J. Neale & Co. The cupboard over drawers may be the most common Shaker case piece form. Scores of variations on the form abound, based on the craftsmen's self assurance and long standing tradition that encouraged a broad array of designs to fit particular needs.

CUPBOARD OVER DRAWERS, WATERVLIET, NEW YORK

New York State Museum

Built by a craftsman who was willing to stretch the acceptable design norms, this piece may have been built by an older, staid Watervliet, New York, Brother secure in his ways. Or, was it made by a younger craftsman, less traditional, possibly newer to the sect? The maker is not known but the exuberant case piece clearly diverges from the traditional "plain and simple" Shaker case piece in its almost brash stance. Three conspicuous design elements stand out. The cornice, a built up complex molding, is notably broader than found in most Shaker pieces, though quite modest compared to those of the Dutch Kas built nearby along the Hudson River. The door panels extend in front of the doors, the opposite of the more common panel that is recessed behind the face of the door and case. Last, and most striking, the robust applied bracket base protrudes unusually from the case. It creates an almost knee-like form extending outwardly to bolster the case like a man's broadly spaced feet provide extra support against a strong wind. The unique base visually counterbalances the broad cornice.

CORNER CUPBOARD, UNION VILLAGE, OHIO

Otterbein Home

Products of vastly different eras, this walnut corner cupboard and the elaborate Victorian building, Marble Hall, originated in the same Shaker community, Union Village, Ohio. They are indicative of Shaker craftsmen's output under vividly different leadership. Products of seemingly different communities, they visually show the complex and dynamic changes that took place. Each stands like a weather vane, unmistakably reflecting the currents of different times. Furniture from the western Shaker communities in Kentucky and Ohio differ little from its worldly kin. Appearing very much like the vernacular furniture in the Mid-west, this refined walnut corner cupboard was beautifully de-signed. A developed sense of proportion exists comfortably between all of its components. Each element – doors and panels, proportions of the feet, and the modest cove-shaped cornice – is integrated well with other design elements, and the whole. Marble Hall was a product of Trustee Joseph Slingerland shown below.

Shaker Museum and Library

CUPBOARDS, MOUNT LEBANON AND WATERVLIET, NEW YORK

Shaker Museum and Library, left photograph by Michael Fredricks

These Shaker cupboards have little in common beyond their red paint and two doors. Clearly crafted by different builders, the first likely built much earlier, ca. 1800, is much more severe. Oriented with one door placed above the other, it sits flat on the floor and has virtually no decorative work, displaying only a minimal bull nose cornice as if placed there out of the coercion of an exacting tradition. This severity though is what makes it a great early piece. The second craftsman placed the double paneled doors side by side, raised and lightened the piece visually by cutting out gracefully shaped arched feet, and completed the case with a tasteful complex decorative cornice. Were the builders simply using their own design prerogative or were they more likely conforming to the strictures of very different periods of Shaker life, one clearly more restrictive than the other? Either way, both pieces are superb examples of a strong Shaker furniture tradition.

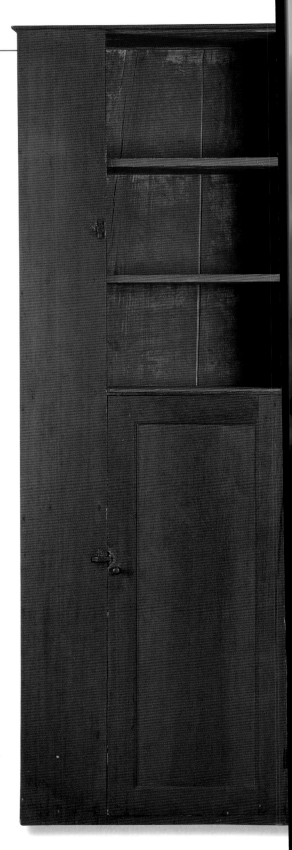

CUPBOARD AND DRAWERS, MOUNT LEBANON, NEW YORK

Hancock Shaker Village

As if built primarily for the sunsets over the herb fields and broad Lebanon valley, the Mount Lebanon community listed to the west on its north south axis. The setting provided "place" for a century and a half for the mother community, where a common faith was shared, in the rituals of their work and worship, in their monastic like separation of brother and sister from the world and its politics, strife, and war. Children brought into the community by their parents became brothers and sisters, elders and eldresses, many living their entire lives set within the community apart from the world. The mountainside setting also provided water, sometimes in excess, trained subterranean in a maze of tunnels for domestic use and waterpower for the shops. With the simple mysteries of waterpower understood and developed, the brothers sawed the logs and with the dried lumber fashioned their furniture. Hundreds of pieces of furniture were built for a wide variety of uses.

This uncharacteristic sill cupboard, one of a pair, was built with the top half of the case recessed from the bottom to create a narrow sill. Though a few others exist, the form is a rarity in Shaker furniture. We do not know where or how this particular cupboard was used. Most likely it was located in an office or workspace where the shallow cupboard space could have been used for books or records. There its original chrome yellow pigmented color would have created a notable presence, like a star in the sky that can't be missed because of its brilliance. The paint has matured or mellowed noticeably over the last 150 years of exposure.

53

CASES OF DRAWERS, MOUNT LEBANON, NEW YORK

Shaker Museum and Library
Private Collection, photograph by
Michael Fredricks, courtesy of
Suzzane Courcier and Robert
Wilkins

These two tall elegant sisters were likely made in the same workshop or in shops within a short walk of each other in the interconnected Mount Lebanon community. The overall design concept, form, and construction are evidence of their close familial relationship. Imbued with robust color, this pair could have been conceived and constructed in a traditional manner with one pair of half width drawers over a bank of drawers. However, the craftsman doubled, then tripled this visual and practical design element, creating more than just a utilitarian piece. A visual balance was created by using a drawer graduation. The larger drawers on the bottom provide visual weight to the massive case pieces, and the smaller banks of half drawers give lightness, balance, and a unique character to such monumental and colorful pieces of furniture. Both were likely built for a brother's or sister's retiring room to a scale larger than typically necessary for a worldly nuclear family.

CASE OF DRAWERS, HANCOCK, MASSACHUSETTS, OR ENFIELD, CONNECTICUT

Hancock Shaker Village

According to a paper label affixed to the interior, this tall butternut case of drawers was a collaborative effort of two known craftsmen, Elder Grove Wright and Brother Thomas Damon. Both held leadership positions within the Hancock bishopric and they were also connected by their skills as craftsmen in wood. Another product of their hands that provided a link with the world that surrounded them was the yarn swift, an intriguing device intended to hold a skein of yarn while it was wound into a ball. Journal entries note years of their collaboration, work of both the hand and the mind that led to a life-long relationship between these two men. Interestingly when Elder Grove, the mentor and older of the two, became too ill to continue in the position of leadership in the Hancock bishopric, Brother Thomas assumed the role.

This Case of Drawers were made by Elder Grove and Brother Thomas and placed here thursday, January 13th, 1853. It was the day our Ministry expected to return to the City of Peace, but were detained on account of the snow storm which occured on that day.

CUPBOARD, SOUTH UNION, KENTUCKY

The Shaker Museum at South Union, Kentucky

Imagine the aroma of the baked goods that wafted throughout the brick dwelling on baking days. How many loaves of bread, pies, or corn bread would have been baked throughout the week for a family of sixty-five believers? Whole kitchens, pantries, and dining rooms were created for the large Shaker families, along with furniture designed for specialized food-related purposes. This cupboard was built for just one of those needs, for short-term food storage and preservation of baked goods. Vernacular and southern influences prevailed through the use of the common tin panels for ventilation in this spectacular piece of western Shaker furniture. It incorporates twenty-four artfully punched tin panels, far more than is typical of a storage cupboard. The craftsman's use of unusual proportion and size bid well for its maker, for at eighty-five inches high the food safe is monumental. Oh, to savor one of those pies or a loaf of hot bread just out of the oven!

Source Unknown

Shaker Museum and Library

Collection of Shaker Museum and Library

Like a pair of drummers playing in perfect time, the visual interplay of structural and design elements in this double bank of drawers was conceived with a perfect, steady rhythm. The craftsman avoided the boredom of simplistic repetition by utilizing the traditional design refinement of a subtle graduation of the drawers. The single bone escutcheon on the top left hand drawer breaks the rhythm like a jazz musician with the nuance of an extra beat, and sets this massive piece apart with a subtle asymmetry.

CASE OF DRAWERS, UNION VILLAGE, OHIO

Art Complex Museum, Duxbury, Massachusetts

Some pieces of furniture owe their greatness to one dominant element. This is one of those pieces. The craftsman's choice of using an outstanding curly maple for this piece sets it apart. The undulating wave of the curly figured wood has a strength and movement and vibrancy rarely found in other surfaces or finishes. This case piece is well built, of fine proportions, and stands in good stead among the best of the western Shaker pieces as well as among those of the more "classic" eastern Shaker forms of the 1830s.

CASE OF DRAWERS, HARVARD, MASSACHUSETTS

Hancock Shaker Village

Once clothed in a bold yellow paint, the hue has changed comfortably over time as homage to generations of use within the Harvard community. This seven-drawer chest was made portable with the addition of handles secured to the wide plank sides. There was rarely the need for moveable furniture in Shaker communities, but travel between communities by the Ministry and certain craftsmen may have precipitated the construction of such pieces. The dovetailed case was constructed separate of the base, allowing it to be lifted free. This afforded some protection to the more fragile base as the chest was moved from one community to another in a horse drawn wagon. The arrangement of the half-width drawers at both the top and bottom of the case is an unusual design characteristic. The carefully arched base and the under slung drawer are also features unique to Harvard craftsmanship. The placement of drawer knobs and the graceful shape of the carrying handles provide an artful relief to the otherwise rigid lines of the case. Ownership, and perhaps crafts-manship, of this piece is known by the inscription on the base: "Thomas Hammond this belongs to his case of draw[er]s." Brother Thomas is known to have traveled frequently between communities, possibly taking this case with him as he traveled.

COUNTER, MOUNT LEBANON, NEW YORK

Mount Lebanon Shaker Collection, photograph by Mark Daniels

A mile long stretch of the Albany to Boston road at the same time connected and separated the various Mount Lebanon families in turn, the North, Church, Second, Center, and South. The proximity of several workshops led to personal and working relationships between craftsmen, encouraging commonality of form and style. Conversely, the separation of the workshops under various leadership styles allowed diversity to develop. This may account for the unusual construction of this long counter finished with a red ochre-pigmented paint. The case construction involves dovetailed joinery between the top, bottom, and the sides, thereby eliminating the long overhanging top found on most Shaker counters. In addition, the case sits directly on the floor, without the relief of feet to lift it off of the floor, a characteristic found early on nineteenth century Shaker furniture.

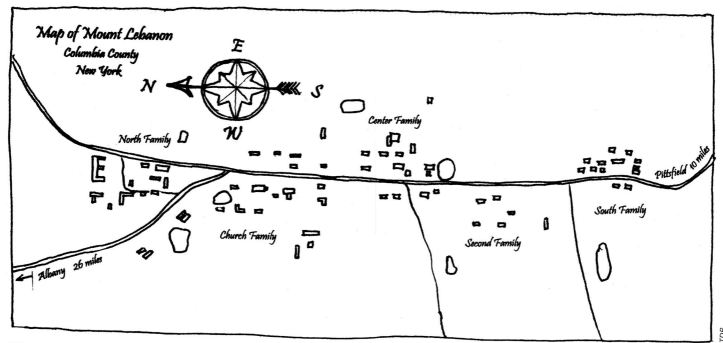

Map of Mount Lebanon
Columbia County
New York

North Family

Center Family

Church Family

Second Family

South Family

Albany 26 miles

Pittsfield 10 miles

TDR

Robert Hamilton, Jr. collection

Certainly among the best examples of Shaker furniture is this curly maple counter. It is not hard to list its many attributes: extremely fine proportions, unique asymmetrical drawer arrangement, exemplary selection of materials, and notable bone escutcheons. Beyond this, though not signed, research collected over the last twenty years has attributed the construction of this piece to Elder Grove Wright or a closely associated craftsman. The use of tapered drawer sides in construction is so unusual, so unique, and almost without exception is associated with craftsmen from the Hancock bishopric. Though one can only speculate on who this counter was built for, it was likely for use by an elder or eldress or someone in the ministry. Another virtually identical counter with the same unique drawer arrangement exists, built entirely in cherry.

Shaker Museum and Library

COUNTER, CANTERBURY, NEW HAMPSHIRE

Shaker Museum and Library

Few pieces of Shaker furniture have a closer connection to the community leadership, the Ministry, than this magnificent counter. According to existing physical evidence and journal references, it was built into the Canterbury meetinghouse pictured here, before 1815. It was used by the Ministry at Canterbury as they worked at the physical labors required of them beyond their ministerial duties. The nearly nine-foot long counter retains its original Prussian blue paint on the case, contrasting with a salmon-orange colored paint on the top. The counters' definitive history is helpful in understanding the early furniture of the Shakers. This counter is one of many used in the crafting of the unique Shaker clothing like that worn by the Canterbury quartet.

COUNTER, CANTERBURY, NEW YORK

**The United Society of Shakers,
Sabbathday Lake, Maine**
    Counters were the work-
benches of the tailor's trade –
large and small, elaborate and
simple, colorful and plain. Tailors,
both men and women, required
furniture with a large work surface
space to lay out and cut fabric for
pants, dresses, shirts, coats, and
cloaks like those shown. The need
for numerous case pieces, in turn,
provided an interesting pallet for
the craftsmen who responded
with unique design solutions. A
craftsman here created what we
have come to appreciate as a
distinct Shaker design, a subtle yet
discernable Shaker asymmetry
with the unique drawer arrangement and unequal drawer widths,
painted yellow, and supported on
a traditional bracket base.

Mark Daniels, The Mount Lebanon Shaker Collection

72

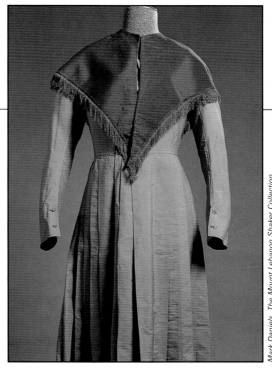

WORK TABLE, CANTERBURY, NEW HAMPSHIRE

Canterbury Shaker Village
A deliberate variation on the Shaker traditions, this unusual worktable exhibits the breadth of Shaker furniture design. Resembling a worldly sideboard in its overall form, no other Shaker worktable like it is known. The design elements – turned posts, overhanging top, the single drop leaf (not visible in the photograph), wheels inset in the posts, and most notably the unusual pairing of long horizontal drawers with the exceptionally deep, nearly square drawers combine to make this a very unique piece. It may have been used as a worktable in the tailor's shop, to facilitate the creation of clothing for the Sisters like that seen in this carefully posed photograph of Canterbury Sisters.

SEWING DESK, CANTERBURY, NEW YORK

Shaker Museum and Library

Shakers' work spaces were often enlivened by the use of bold color on furniture and interior wood work. Shakers rarely utilized decorative paint, that is, the manipulation of the surface of the wet paint to emulate a fancy wood grain. They did make use of boldly painted wood, beautifully contrasted with the subtle warmth of varnished wood. The now mottled red paint was a much more vibrant red when the desk was first carried into the Sisters' workroom over a century ago. Many earlier sewing desks were finished in a strong red or yellow color. Sisters' work spaces in particular must have been visually alive with the combinations of colorful woodwork, various desks and tables, the mixture of fabrics, and the movement of the Sisters at work. Though neither Brother Benjamin Smith nor Henry Blinn built this particular desk, they built several, and were a part of a cadre of skilled woodworkers in the Canterbury community who built the distinctive, now classic, Shaker sewing desk.

Collection of Richard Brooker

DESK, ENFIELD, NEW HAMPSHIRE

Miller collection, Hancock Shaker Village

Unfortunately only the façade, the exterior of a piece of furniture, is what is seen by most, like a functional sculpture, seen only in the present. So much is missed not knowing and experiencing the creation of the piece, the building process. There is so much that is not visible in a piece such as this one. The case is essentially of post and beam, or stile and rail, construction similar to that of a building, the horizontal and vertical parts secured with mortise and tenon joints. Loose panels were captured in grooves in the framework, with a top and work surface added to complete the exterior of the piece. A complex of interior support work was added to support and guide the drawers, interior, and structure of the desk. A surprising 100 glue blocks were secreted into the structure, the cabinetmaker supplementing the already strong traditional framework. Yet even with an understanding of the structure of the desk, many other aspects are not known.

What was the mindset of the builder, a sense of contentment, creation, or frustration? What were the problems with the piece, the changes, and possible errors? In the end we are left with only the existence of the piece itself, with all of the questions one may have about it. Who built it and who used it? The questions go on. There are more questions than answers about this piece that appears to be an unusual aberration in the Shaker sewing desk form. Designed possibly as a writing desk with its slanted leather bound writing surface, this painted piece is somewhat larger than the typical sewing desk. Breaking from the visual honesty expected in Shakers work, the façade is unusual and beyond the norm, as the drawers on the front right are actually immobile false drawer fronts placed there apparently to visually balance the piece. The three small drawers on the back of the case are unique.

79

SEWING DESK, WATERVLIET, NEW YORK

Photograph courtesy of John Keith Russell
Private collection

Change within the sect was never so poignant as was portrayed in the late nineteenth and early twentieth century photographs of the Shakers. The previous gender balance within the sect had markedly changed to the dominance of sisters. Feminism was taken up by many sisters and espoused in one of the Shakers periodicals, *The Shaker and Shakeress*. The publication of *Shakerism: Its Meaning and Message* by two sisters, Anna White and Leila S. Taylor, recorded and may have promoted a renewed Sister strength.

Their numbers and strength provided considerable income through a variety of community industries. Though most furniture was made for mixed gender use, the sewing desk was one form made particularly for women's use. Little furniture is more specialized. While some details of this desk clearly resemble other Shaker sewing desks, the craftsman's interpretation of the form is distinctive. It was designed to meet the same fundamental needs, with a work surface, gallery of small drawers, and unique drawer storage space built into the base, and follows the same basic frame and panel construction. Yet this interpretation is dramatically different. The builder of this piece altered the more traditional design, eliminated the use of turned legs, and incorporated only linear, rectangular forms in his clean spare design. Faced with the task of meeting particular needs a yet unknown, the Shaker craftsman created a unique desk.

1. Anna White
2. Elizabeth Cantrell
3. Emma Neale, Carrie Wade, Sadie Neale
4. Sarah Berger
5. Catherine Allen
6. Canterbury sisters

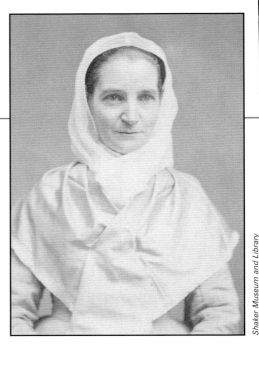

Shaker Museum and Library

Hancock Shaker Village

W.G.C. Kimball, Hancock Shaker Village

SEWING DESK AND ARMLESS ROCKER, ENFIELD, CONNECTICUT

Shaker Museum and Library
Private collection

The spectacular random beauty of birds eye maple is in reality an accident or oddity in nature caused by a unknown source in the hard maple tree. Furniture rarely displays the vibrant visual strength and power primarily through one isolated aspect of its design, the exquisite selection of materials like in this Victorian sewing desk and armless rocker. The craftsmen had at hand different design elements of composition, form, color, materials, and knew intuitively that a proper integration of these elements can supplement or detract from the overall piece. Here the birds eye maple dominates but enhances the piece, providing a colorful unity and strength in the overall composition. Within this desk the craftsman clearly resolved the argument among many Shaker enthusiasts over a century later, of the "plain and simple" versus the inroads of Victorianism, what the Shakers earlier may have called "superflousness". The craftsman followed the well-traveled footpath of Shaker design traditions, yet carefully and successfully piggybacked Victorian decoration within the piece. It certainly appears that he was seeking a new visual reality rather than grimly holding on to the old Shaker ways. The soul continues to exist, yet at times, wears new attire.

Numerous historic photographs show the interior aesthetics of retiring and work rooms clearly had changed toward the last quarter of the nineteenth century. In what were previously sparsely decorated rooms and unadorned white walls, according to mid-nineteenth century descriptions, one can see walls appointed with photographs, calendars, advertisements or paintings. Some within the community expressed their frustration regarding change within the Shaker society. In his assessment of the times, and specifically their

products, Brother Orren Haskins, a prolific New Lebanon furniture maker expresses, perhaps, his personal agony in seeing the changes around him.

Why patronize the out side world or gugaws [sic] in our manufactures, when they will say we have enough of them abroad? We want a good plain substantial Shaker article, yea, one that bears credit to our profession & tells who and what we are, true and honest before the world, without hypocrisy or any false covering. The wourld [sic] at large can Scarcely keep pace with its self in its stiles and fassions [sic] which last but a short time, when something still more worthless or absurd takes its place. Let good enough alone, and take good common sense for our guide in al [sic] our pursuits, and we are safe within and without.

82

SEWING TABLE GROVELAND, NEW YORK

Canterbury Shaker Village

Sister Ester Marion Kate Scott is seated near this or a similar sewing desk, another example of a craftsman's unique interpretation of a common form, the sewing table. It is unclear what the design sources were for the piece that is more reminiscent of the arts and crafts style built decades later, than the tapered leg Federal period tables that were prototypes of earlier sewing or work tables. A variety of small details contribute to its exquisite and successful design. The rounded thumbnail edge on the stiles that surround the gallery drawers and the ovolo-shaped corners on the work surfaces, enhance what might otherwise have been an overly rigid, rectilinear piece. The Victorian brass and porcelain knobs, purchased from the world, were given visual prominence by raising the knob above the drawer face on a chamfered pyramid pedestal, providing an unexpected visual crescendo like the musical elaboration of romantic composers Tchaikovsky or Brahms of the same period.

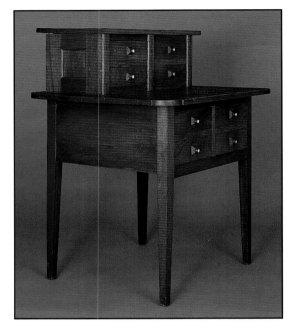

Private collection

84

New York State Museum

85

SEWING DESK, HANCOCK, MASSACHUSETTS

Hancock Shaker Village

The dominance of either male or female leadership within the communities may have swung one way or another depending upon the strengths of particular brothers or sisters assuming leadership roles. Roles were, as in the society at large, often gender specific. Men dominated the work in the fields, women in the kitchen, though formally, they assumed equal and parallel leadership in most areas, from economic to spiritual. The overall Shaker administrative structure was a hierarchy, a top down organization most often male led, where many aspects of physical design were regulated by the Lead Ministry. Despite this, each community seemed to take creative liberties. The round stone barn at Hancock was one such example, a magnificent stone structure as well known in the 1840s agricultural community when it housed dozens of dairy cattle, as it is known now in the architectural community and as a tourist attraction. Shaker furniture craftsman as well took liberties in their creations. The unique style of sewing desk in the Hancock bishopric differed from those built in other communities. This four drawer case piece is one example, a small rectangular case of drawers built in cherry. They were usually wider than high and built without the gallery commonly found on sewing desks made in the Mount Lebanon and Canterbury communities. The number and arrangements of drawers vary widely on the fifteen to twenty known sewing desks. Many also carry a drop leaf hinged to the back edge of the top to expand the work surface.

SEWING TABLE WITH GALLERY, MOUNT LEBANON, NEW YORK

Hancock Shaker Village

Situated in the center of many historic photographs was the Shaker sewing table or desk surrounded by Shaker sisters. Many were built in response to a dynamic economy in the Shaker community. By the mid-nineteenth century, the emphasis on the agricultural products waned. With an increasingly female membership, the sewing trades grew exponentially, accounting for a larger income in Shaker communities. This particular cherry table was built ca. 1830 with the gallery added in 1881 by Brother Orren Haskins. With fine proportions and slender tapered legs, it was the form most common to Mount Lebanon. Utilizing tables like this one, the Sisters plied their skills, creating a myriad of small handicrafts for sale to tourists up and down the East Coast as well as to those who visited Shaker communities. The "fancy goods" industries were so popular that a small brochure, *Products of Intelligence and Diligence,* was printed to offer some of these articles, like the spool holder shown, to a wider audience.

PRODUCTS of
INTELLIGENCE
and DILIGENCE

SHAKERS Church Family
MOUNT LEBANON Col. Co.
NEW YORK

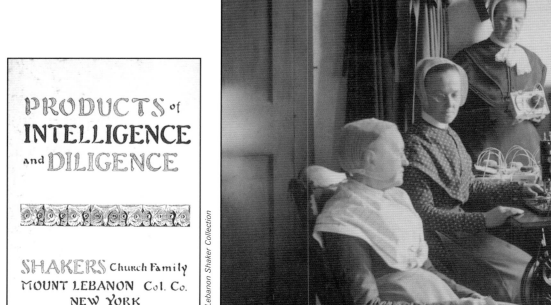

The Mount Lebanon Shaker Collection

Hancock Shaker Village

These graceful washstands speak to the design skill of their creator, Abner Allen. It is unclear whether washstands stood in the retiring rooms, hallways, or other specifically designed areas, but it is evident that there were many of them to meet the hygiene needs of a communal family. There are several striking features in these pieces: one is dated a rather late 1850, yet the doors retain the raised panel construction of an earlier era; the drawers exhibit the distinctive tapered sides; the gallery sides are all slightly flared, and the height of the back splashboard gives a visual lift to an otherwise heavier rectilinear piece of furniture. Finally, that there are two nearly identical pieces speaks to the possibility of more of them. What was it about the Enfield community that supported and encouraged the particularly fascinating and fine craftsmanship of Brother Abner?

Shaker Museum and Library

Private collection

This exquisite table displays the distinctive drawer joinery marked by the use of tapered drawer sides, uniquely known to the Hancock bishopric. The piece's overall elegance is enhanced by the combination of a slightly flared gallery, beautifully turned legs, and the use of figured maple. The table, which may have been used by brothers or sisters shown here from Enfield, is attributed to Shaker craftsman Abner Allen, who wedded superb technical and design skills. He clearly understood his trade; his joinery and dovetail work are impeccable, but the piece is not signed. One can only speculate why some pieces are signed and others are not. Numerous Shaker craftsmen, well documented in the book *Shaker Furniture Makers* by Jerry Grant and Douglas Allen, signed their furniture, among them Amos Stewart, Abner Allen, Eli Kidder, Benjamin Lyon, and possibly most often Orren Haskins. Brother Orren often chronicled his furniture. At the age of seventeen, he signed a table OH 1833, and often seemingly proudly signed a piece in a outspoken penciled script three or four inches high. Did some craftsmen have the need to be known beyond those who knew them personally? Did they want their identity and work to go beyond their generation, beyond anonymity? Was it an issue of pride or vanity? The (1845) Rules spoke to the issue. Objects should not be signed. At any rate, fortunately for students of the field, historians, and curators, the rule was often broken.

Hancock Shaker Village

Left Photograph by Michael Fredricks, courtesy of Suzzane Courcier and Robert J. Wilkins
Private collections

Give two seasoned furniture makers from two eastern Shaker communities washstand specifications, each with their own workshop and community traditions, strictures, and a craftsman's latitude, and see what the results are. Here are two very creative products, superb responses to the needs of two communities, Enfield, New Hampshire, and Hancock, Massachusetts. Each displays an overhanging gallery placed atop a rectangular frame and paneled base on turned legs. The overall size and proportion, choice in the use of drawers and/ or cupboard doors, and the application of color lead to two very colorful, functional, and different products. Neither of the two craftsmen who built these pieces, nor information beyond a general community attribution, is presently known. No written signatures exist. Yet most craftsmen left signatures of sorts, sometimes an overall manner or style of work, or a particular way of making a joint. The tapered drawer sides of the Hancock bishopric, or the peculiar breadboard ends on Mount Lebanon blanket boxes, or the distinctive Victorian furniture of Brother Henry Green are signatures or "trademarks". Often careful examination is necessary to see the repeated overcuts of a craftsman's dovetail joinery or the style of the numbers for drawer parts layout that may lead to a clear maker identification. Others not signed can be grouped or identified as one of a family linage, blood relatives or more distant cousins identified by their similarities. Some pieces though are inscrutable, withholding mysteries that may never be solved.

TRIPOD STANDS, ENFIELD, CONNECTICUT, AND MOUNT LEBANON, NEW YORK

Private collections

Shaker tripod stands run the design gamut in their basic form and finishing details. On the left, this snake leg stand from Enfield has unique detail turnings on the pedestal, just above where the legs are dovetailed into the post. A slightly bulbous turned stem supports an elegant top with ovolo corners and a pair of under hung drawers. On the right, the round top stand is stamped SISTER ASNETH/ELD.S.RUTH, marked for Sister Aseneth Clark and Eldress Ruth Landon. It is attributed to Brother Samuel Humphrey Turner. This table is well designed; the larger stem and dimension of its spider-leg mirrors that of the round top. The gracefully turned stem moves from a full base to a finer stem at the top, giving the table an uncharacteristic visual weight. Shaker craftsmen produced stands with both styles of leg. These tables are each clearly identifiable as Shaker built, but they represent notably different interpretations of the tripod base form.

TRESTLE TABLE, HANCOCK, MASSACHUSETTS, AND WATERVLIET, NEW YORK

Shaker Museum and Library
Private collection, photograph
courtesy of John Keith
Russell

Many brothers and sisters alike were involved in the production of food, its preparation, preservation, and marketing. For the consumption of food prepared for community members, it was no mistake that Shakers chose the trestle table form to best accommodate their communal dining. With the table legs centrally located and no apron under the top, they are more comfortable and convenient for seating. Shaker trestle tables varied in length and design of the base. Most tables had arched feet, joined to a vertical rectangular or turned post with a cleat affixed on it to support the top. Designs in the foot and the post varied remarkably between communities. The longer table illustrated is from Hancock, the form dominated by the central turned member, which reflects the turned posts in the Church Family dining room. The smaller table is from Watervliet, New York, with each part of the base sculpted from flat curly maple stock. The historic view emphasizes the number and size of tables needed for the large Shaker family dining rooms where their meals were consumed in silence.

99

Canterbury Shaker Village

Long work tables served a variety of uses within the Shaker community. They were found in tailoring shops, herb processing rooms, bake rooms, and ironing rooms like in the historic photograph in Mount Lebanon illustrated here. Furniture destined for workshop use often displayed a sense of dignity and strength in the integral design, in fact they were often among the best of the furniture because their particularly rugged or robust character. Here details like the unusual large cove molding under the top, the heavy drawer rail under the three drawers, the mass of the table leg and the corner joinery, and the muscular nearly organic turnings of the table leg convey a quiet visceral strength (like an ancient Roman sculpture). The choice of a painted finish pulled the various elements together to create a particularly functional and handsome table.

BLANKET CHESTS, ENFIELD, NEW HAMPSHIRE, AND HARVARD, MASSACHUSETTS

**Collection and Photograph
    Robert Hamilton, Jr., Hancock
    Shaker Village**
    Color may be the most
significant design factor separating these two blanket boxes, one from Enfield, New Hampshire, the other from Harvard. There are numerous design details that differentiate them, size, number of drawers, proportion, the use of panels on the lid, edge molding styles, the single escutcheon, and the unique addition of the underhung drawer. But in the end, one inevitably returns to one of the important tenants of Shaker design, the almost lavish use of color as the primary factor. Imagine the change of any space with the addition of either of these storage chests.

BLANKET CHEST, MOUNT LEBANON, NEW YORK

Shaker Museum and Library

Tempered over time to a much thinner muted color, the chrome yellow paint is still strong. The use of painted furniture such as this blanket chest may have made the early nineteenth century Shaker residences much more colorful than most of our twenty-first century homes. Several of these two drawer blanket chests are known in either red or yellow paint. Each uses the cut foot base that necessitates a simple nailed case construction rather than the more common dovetailed case joinery. The vertical grain orientation of the end of the case allows for the cut foot. The foot on the front was integrated into the bottom rail with a beveled joint. Another unique identifiable feature of many Mt. Lebanon blanket boxes is the bread board end with the integral molded lip. This eliminated the need for the often troublesome continuous molding around the hinged top, and provided a finishing touch unique to Mount Lebanon blanket boxes.

Robert J. Wilkins

Robert J. Wilkins

Photograph by Michael Fredricks, courtesy of Suzanne Courcier and Robert J. Wilkins
Private Collection

Known affectionately as the Cyclops, with its centrally located single top drawer, this blanket box is extraordinary. As if marching to a different drummer, an unknown craftsman created this regal piece. Few Shaker blanket boxes have more than two or three drawers, four or five drawers would be rare; one, other than this example, is presently known with more. Even without the small ninth drawer, this tall blanket box is simply unique; trying, it seems, to pose as both a blanket box and a tall case of drawers. It certainly served as both. It is well built, with a fine proportionate spacing and graduation of drawers, and set on a well fashioned tall ogee shaped bracket base found on other case pieces made in the Enfield, New Hampshire, community.

Hancock Shaker Village

107

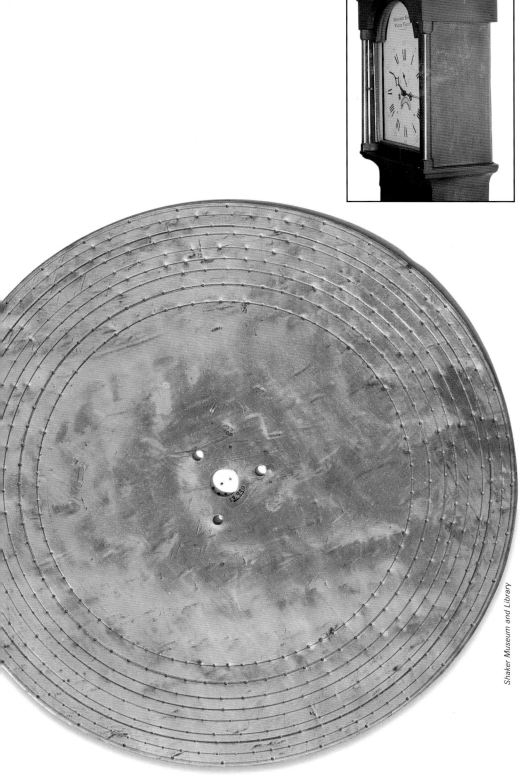

The Mount Lebanon Shaker Collection, photograph by Mark Daniels

In near perfection, the clock's pendulum regulated pallet quietly tiptoed its way around the escape wheel, rhythmically marking the still air with its dignified sound. A radically different interpretation of the sound and presence of a clock in a Shaker room was recorded by Charles Dickens in a visit to Mount Lebanon. "We walked into a grim room where several grim hats were hanging on grim pegs and the time was grimly told by a grim clock which uttered every tick with a kind of struggle, as if it broke the grim silence reluctantly and under protest..." Was this response, indelibly etched into Charles Dickens mind, provoked in a room with this particular clock? We will never know, though Dickens negative sentiment is obvious. So often the description of objects or events becomes "history", assumed incorrectly to be an objective record with little or no indication of the observer's presence or bias.

Housed in this cherry tall clock case is the heart of the clockmaker's craft, the clock movement. The movement can be exposed with the removal of the bonnet, revealing a marvel of eighteenth and nineteenth century technology and precision. The cast brass plates provided a foundation for the precision parts, the pinions, clock wheels, and escape wheel. The turned parts were carefully machined by hand in the small clockmakers lathe, showing a gauged precision. Each individual tooth on each clock wheel was cut one at a time on the tooth cutting engine, then indexed ahead incrementally for the next tooth to be cut. Other parts within the time and strike mechanism were accurately cast and filed, the mating parts polished to allow a near frictionless running. Brother Benjamin's brass clock movements and appropriately simplified casework show an integration of his training by his father as a Connecticut clockmaker, and his accommodation of the Shaker way of life.

Private collections

The degree of artistic angularity differentiates the Shaker plank bottom chair from its worldly predecessor. The chair maker took the design element seriously, taking the form well beyond simple function. The leg angle creates an angle wider than the norm, perhaps exaggerated somewhat by the high placement of the rungs. The angularity is complemented and contrasted by the rounded seat surface as seen from the top. The design is consummated with the sharp front edge that beautifully reflects the chair's carefully developed design. Benches, literal extensions of the chair, were made for meeting-house use. Many observers today seeing the red painted, low back chairs quip about how uncomfortable they look, as a child complains about the taste of food never having tried it. They were distinct improvements over the long benches they replaced.

111

ROCKING CHAIR, HARVARD, MASSACHUSETTS

Private collection

Occasionally what characterizes the best of Shaker furniture is the builder's ability to take a particular idea to the extreme. Or it may be something more fundamental, taking the concept or design back to the basics, with the use of scale, repetition, or fine proportions. This fine chair encompasses both. Visually a tall, lanky, angularity defines the strength of this chair. The long slender turnings in curly maple, four rather than three back slats, and the strong slant defined by the precise placement of the rocker creating an exaggerated lean to the rear, are combined to create an unusual but fine chair. The broad rocker is uncommon as is the addition of the rocker extension created for the safety of the user. Armless rockers may have been built initially as work chairs, as inadvertently shown in this historic photograph, rather than for leisure use. The rocker allowed easy repositioning when doing handwork at a table or in search of the best light by a lamp or window.

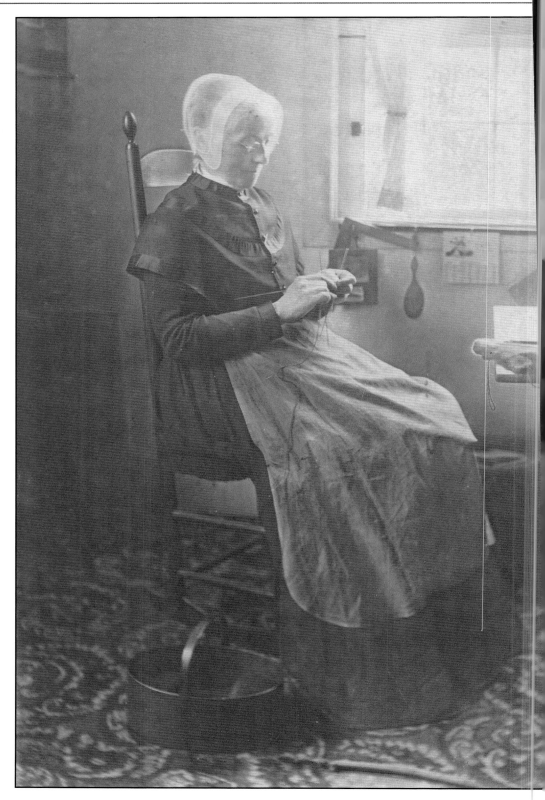

SIDE CHAIR WITH TILTERS, MOUNT LEBANON, NEW YORK

Shaker Museum and Library

This figured birch chair is one of a small group of particularly exquisite chairs made by a Mt. Lebanon chair maker, likely brother Geo. O'Donnell, or someone who worked in his shadow. The 'flame' birch used in this chair is much less common than curly or tiger maple. The undulating figure, a broadly rolling grain is spaced much wider than curly maple, and reflects light from the patterned diagonal grain configuration. A majority of these chairs were fitted with brass three part brass ball and socket tilters patented by Brother George. This is the only one known, however, to have a cast pewter tilter rather than brass or the much more common turned wooden ball and socket mechanism. The seat rails are specially shaped and drilled for a light resilient cane seat.

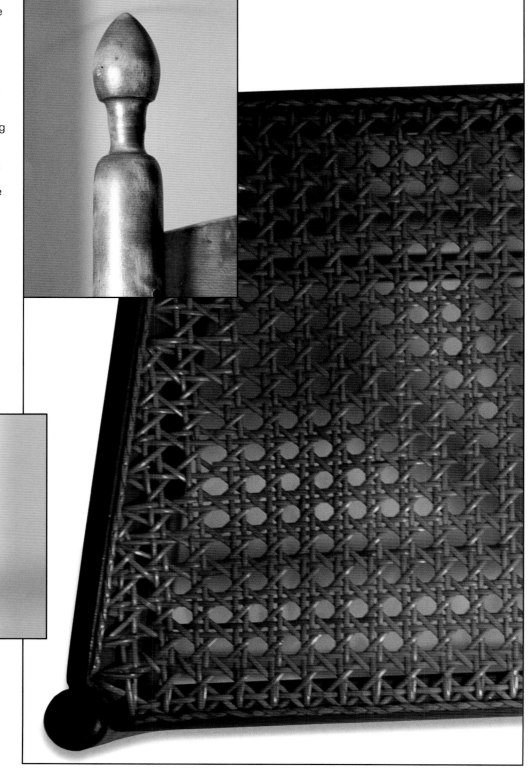

CHAIR SEATING

Listing, the hand woven wool seating material used on most Shaker chairs, was made in the early days by the sisters. They were veritable twenty to thirty-five yard long tapestries 5/8 to 1 1/4 wide, some colors were "dyed in the wool", the individual wool fibers carded, then given their color in the dye maker's kettles using formulas recorded in the beautifully penned dye maker's recipe books. Others were likely first twisted into strong threads as they were drawn onto the smooth steel spindle of the large wool spinning wheels before being dyed. The loom was warped, the colored threads systematically organized according the weaver's scripted patterns, the weft then methodically woven, crossing the warp, right to left-left to right, again and again on the small wooden looms. In time with numerous rolls of listing accumulated, they were woven again, usually in a simple checkerboard pattern, over the chair frame with additional padding placed between the layers of tightly woven fabric; all this to provide simple comfortable seating for the Shaker chair. By the 1870s though, this beautifully woven and colored variegated tape was replaced by commercially produced, usually single color, cotton tape. Thousands of chairs were produced, requiring many swift hands to seat them. Sister Sarah Collins was well known in this role, as she posed for several wonderful photographs seating chairs over several decades.

Noel Vicentini, Private collection

117

SIDE CHAIR, CANTERBURY, NEW HAMPSHIRE

Collection and photograph Robert Hamilton, Jr. collection

The side chairs of the Canterbury bishopric have long been considered the most elegant of the Shakers chairs. This example from Canterbury is much rarer and matches them for simple elegance. The chair differs in subtle ways. The pommel or finial is more bulbous in shape than those from Enfield and shows the turners finesse and design sense. The back slats are broad and notably graduated and are slotted into slender posts. Tilter balls and cane seating complete a finely proportioned and well-built chair. The front post bears the # 18 that designates its use for the Elder brothers retiring room in the Canterbury church family dwelling. The elder brothers pictured are from Canterbury.

CHAIRS, MOUNT LEBANON, NEW YORK

**Shaker Museum and Library,
Photograph by Michael
Fredricks**

Measured by a different scale,
the internationally known production chair is arguably one of the
Shaker masterpieces. Certainly it
was a success story, a master-
piece of marketing. The chairs
may have been rather modernis-
tic, good candidates for the
"Nineteenth Century Modern"
book. Built of dark stained maple,
they had a clean look with simple
curvilinear lines, and a comfortable woven seat. A touch of the
Victorian excess was added to
some with colorful, extravagant
plush cushions. Sister Lillian
Barlow was among the last to
build the Shakers' chairs. In the
half-century since her death, the
chairs have been in the realm of
collectors, antique dealers, and
contemporary craftsmen building
reproductions of the Shakers lean,
functional product.

Shaker Museum and Library

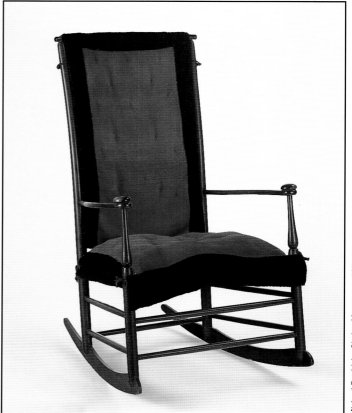

Michael Fredricks, Shaker Museum and Library

REVOLVING CHAIR, MOUNT LEBANON, NEW YORK

New York State Museum,
Hancock Shaker Village

In an 1860 diary entry, Elder James Prescott registered his surprise regarding a revolving chair, referring to it as "a new kind of chair which turns on a screw pivot every which way". The concept and design were apparently new to Elder James and to the Shakers product line of chairs that were developed and sold by Robert Wagan. The concept was certainly not invented by the Shakers; they did, however, develop it for a variety of specific uses. The central moving part of most of the revolvers was a unique, gracefully shaped cast iron four fingered yoke, supported on a long screw captured in a nut below. This simple mechanism allowed the seat to "pivot every which way". The best-known revolver utilizes a turned, slightly hallowed seat above a tapered stem secured on a half-lapped band sawed spider legs below providing a stable base. Bent back spindles were tenoned into the turned seat and boldly curved back rail. The Shakers followed with a myriad of designs though, from the perspectives of the blacksmith, with a simple iron spider base, to a more complex Windsor chair maker's four-leg base.

ARM CHAIR, SABBATHDAY LAKE, MAINE

The United Society of Shakers, Sabbathday Lake, Maine
Diverging dramatically from the traditional Shaker ladder back form, Brother Delmar Wilson's interpretation of the Morris chair speaks eloquently to his knowledge and sense of design. It also reflects his fine craftsmanship, his willingness to move from the Shaker tradition, and beautifully reflects the craftsman's acceptance to inevitable change in Shaker society as a whole. The chair speaks to the openness to comfort and relaxation, and possibly the change in the demographics, the aging population of the Shaker community.

MEETING ROOM BENCH, MOUNT LEBANON, NEW YORK

The Mount Lebanon Shaker Collection, photograph by Mark Daniels

Mirroring other obvious changes within the Shaker communities, this meeting room bench was made for the Shakers by a Gardner, Massachusetts, firm. It may be most important in a symbolic sense completing the story of Shaker furniture as there were too few Shaker brothers still working in wood to accommodate the community's needs after a disastrous fire. Shaker design, a quiet part of an all encompassing ideology or theology, moved from the Shaker built severe case piece with virtually no decorative work to this Victorian bench modestly emulating the world's excesses. Nearly a full circle was completed from independence, near defiance of the world, to a position of more accommodation and acceptance. Fewer or different lines of demarcation between Shakers and the world were made. Within the declining community reminiscence may have been more fervent than the visions of the future.

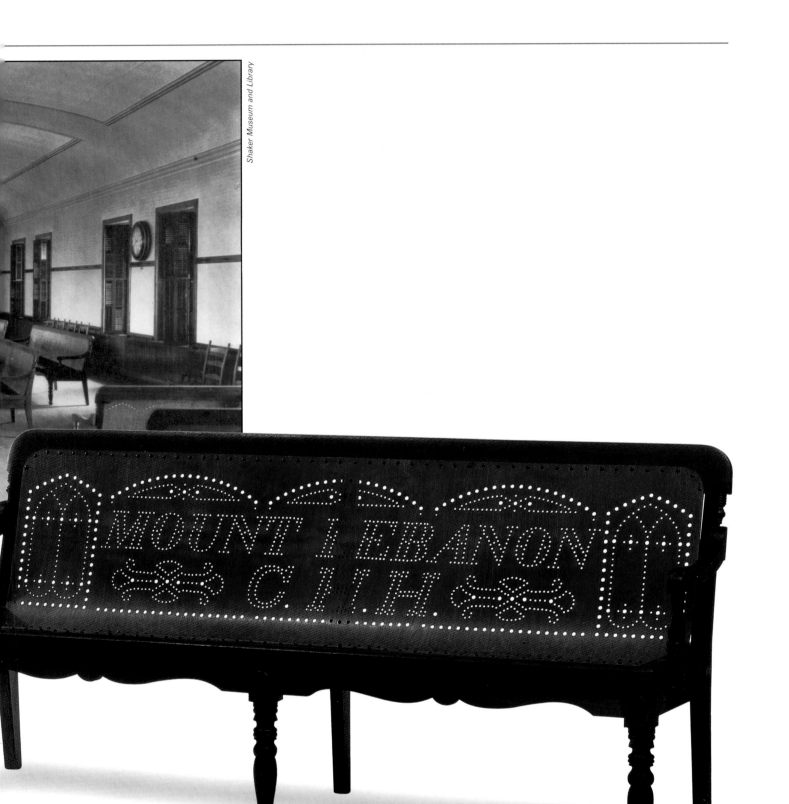

127